The Aquinas Lecture, 1981

RHYME AND REASON
St. Thomas and
Modes of Discourse

Under the auspices of the
Wisconsin-Alpha Chapter of Phi Sigma Tau

By
RALPH McINERNY

MARQUETTE UNIVERSITY PRESS
MILWAUKEE
1981

Library of Congress Catalog Number 81-80234

© Copyright 1981
Marquette University

ISBN 0-87462-148-8

To My Father

CONTENTS

Prefatory

The Wisconsin-Alpha Chapter of Phi Sigma Tau, the National Honor Society for Philosophy at Marquette University, each year invites a scholar to deliver a lecture in honor of St. Thomas Aquinas.

The 1981 Aquinas Lecture *Rhyme and Reason: St. Thomas and Modes of Discourse* was delivered in the Todd Wehr Chemistry Building on Sunday, February 22, 1981, by Ralph M. McInerny, the Michael P. Grace Professor of Medieval Studies at the University of Notre Dame, Notre Dame, Indiana.

After completing his undergraduate studies at St. Paul Seminary, Dr. McInerny earned a M.A. at the University of Minnesota and a Ph.L. and a Ph.D. at Université Laval. After a year at the Creighton University, he began his teaching career at Notre Dame in 1955 where he became Professor of Philosophy in 1969. Since 1978 he has been the Michael P. Grace Professor of Medieval Studies at Notre Dame as well as Director of both the Jacques Maritain Center and the Medieval Institute. After having served as Associate Editor for ten years, he became Editor of *The New Scholasticism* in 1976.

Since 1967 Dr. McInerny has published fourteen novels and has delighted mystery fans with his Father Dowling stories. In Philosophy his books include: *The Logic of Analogy: An Interpretation of St. Thomas* (1961), *From the Beginnings of Philosophy to Plotinus* (1963), *Thomism in an Age of Renewal* (1966), *Studies in Analogy* (1968), *Philosophy from St. Augustine to Ockham* (1970), and *St. Thomas Aquinas* (1977). His published articles in books and journals number over fifty.

Dr. McInerny received an Honorary Doctor of Letters Degree from St. Benedict College in 1978. He served as President of the American Catholic Philosophical Association in 1971-2 and is a member of over a dozen medieval, philosophical, and literary associations.

To Professor McInerny's distinguished list of publications, Phi Sigma Tau is pleased to add: *Rhyme and Reason: St. Thomas and Modes of Discourse*.

RHYME AND REASON
St. Thomas and Modes of Discourse

Prologue

I think it was Collingwood who re-
marked that the oldest extant historical
document refers wistfully to the good old
days, gone alas like our youth too soon.
So too, already in the Fourth Century B.C.,
Plato spoke of an ancient quarrel between
poetry and philosophy. If it is an old one,
it is also, to say the least, an odd quarrel.
By any account, Plato is one of the most
poetic philosophers, not only because of
the literary achievement the dialogues are
universally recognized as being, but also
because of the myths he fashioned to carry
the burden of his most cherished tenets.

Furthermore, Socrates, the main char-
acter in so many of the dialogues, is repre-
sented awaiting execution in his cell, writ-
ing poetry, something he does in response
to a divine call. Likewise, Boethius, at the
opening of *The Consolation of Philosophy*,
unjustly condemned to death, has given

himself over to the poetic muses. These questionable ladies are driven from the cell by Dame Philosophy who sternly advises Boethius to seek comfort in more substantial stuff, namely philosophy. Yet Dame Philosophy often expresses herself in verse as she administers the needed therapy. Whatever the opposition between philosophy and poetry is meant to be, it clearly is not an easy one to characterize.

The issue is not clarified by noticing the supposed antiquity of the quarrel and consulting Plato's predecessors. One of the most noteworthy things about Greek philosophy is that it went on for generations before it began to express itself in prose. It did not go from bad to verse but perhaps the other way around. The fragments of the Pre-Socratic philosophers that have come down to us are, by and large, in poetic form. It is true that we find Heraclitus criticizing the views of the theological poets, but it is the doctrine, not the poetry, that is his target. So too with Plato the quarrel turns on the false and demeaning things the poets have said of the gods, a charge which raises questions about the way in which a poem means and the manner in which it may be said to be true—or false.

However obscure the quarrel can seem, it is perennially renewed. Philosophers often dismiss arguments, positions, pieces of discourse, as poetic, as pretty but imprecise, perhaps even meaningless. The poet functions as a sort of frothing dithyrambic foil for the philosopher. "Bards tell many a lie," Aristotle quotes, and it is unmistakable that he takes his own efforts to be a corrective not only of those predecessors he recognizes as philosophers but also of theological poetry and myth as well. My distinguished predecessor in this lecture series, Professor Victor M. Hamm, had many important and illuminating things to say on this topic.[1] If I presume to take it up anew in this place it is with the sense of depending upon and adding to what he had to say. John of Salisbury quotes Bernard of Chartres to the effect that we are dwarfs who stand on the shoulders of giants and thus see farther than they did. I prefer T. S. Eliot's variation on this in "Tradition and the Individ-

ual Talent." Eliot imagines a critic asking
why we should read the old writers since
we know so much more than they did.
"Yes," he replies, "and they are what we
know."

What I propose to do in this lecture is,
first, to examine the ancient quarrel in its
ancient setting, with particular reference
to Aristotle. Next I will turn to an examina-
tion of what St. Thomas can teach us on
this matter. I end with some suggestions
about the style of philosophy that are
meant to be of significance for its sub-
stance as well.

1. *An Ancient Quarrel*

It is well known that Aristotle had a way
of beginning his treatises with an account
of what his predecessors had to say about
the questions he intends to address. It is
equally well known that Aristotle con-
siders what he has to say as marking a
significant advance over his predecessors'
doctrine. That is, there is a contrast sug-
gested between adequate and inadequate
philosophy. But what would be the con-

trast between philosophy and non-philoso-
phy? What criteria enable us to identify
discourse as philosophical discourse?

One contrast very prominent in both
Plato and Aristotle is that between the
philosopher and the Sophist. To philoso-
phize is to be in pursuit of wisdom and
ultimately of such knowledge of the divine
as is possible for mortal man. For the
Greeks, philosophy was not a career but
a vocation, a way of life. The tribe of
Sophists was the target both of Plato's
rhetorical invective and of Aristotle's more
dispassionate analysis of their arguments.
Although their approaches to the Sophist
differed, Plato and Aristotle agreed in
thinking that the trouble with the Sophist
was in large part a moral one. Doing it for
money is symptomatic of something far
worse. The Sophist was only pretending
to do something; he was mimicking or
parodying something of whose importance
neither Plato nor Aristotle had the slight-
est doubt. The Sophist was pretending to
be wise. Really to be wise is to love wis-
dom, to seek it all the days of one's life
and for itself alone. Unlike Lady Anne

Gregory, of whom Yeats wrote that "only God could love you for yourself alone and not your yellow hair," Lady Wisdom is the terminal object of desire. Seeking wisdom is the whole point of life; it is in that that human perfection and happiness consist. The term "philosophy" conveys the sense and purpose of life, the fundamental ordination of the human person to a felicific and aretaic goal.

Notice that the charge against the Sophist is not that he said what is not true. A conceptual mistake, an error in thought, is not, just as such, a moral fault. The charge against the Sophist is not simply that what he says is false, though that too is involved; rather and more profoundly the charge is that the Sophist knows this and does not care. The difference is that between saying something false and deceiving, telling a lie. By contrast, the philosopher, in seeking wisdom, is held to moral rectitude and, again in different ways, both Plato and Aristotle insist on the connection between moral and intellectual virtue. Here then is a first sense of non-philosophy: Sophistry.

Neither Plato nor Aristotle would contrast philosophy with either mathematics or natural science. These and other disciplines and arts are necessary for the being or well-being of wisdom. The order of learning that St. Thomas gleaned from various passages of Aristotle went like this: first one should learn logic, then mathematics, then natural philosophy, then moral philosophy and finally what we have come to call metaphysics.[2] A not wholly dissimilar paideia can be descried in the *Republic*. The regimen of the philosopher was intellectual and moral; it embraced a plurality of practises and disciplines teleologically ordered to such knowledge as men could attain of the divine. And the appropriate expression of that culminating knowledge was contemplation.

What then, aside from Sophistry, is excluded? In the *Poetics* we are told (1451b1) that poetry is more philosophical and serious than history. Surely this suggests that both history and poetry can be contrasted with philosophy. The reason for the ranking is that poetry deals with universals and history with particu-

lars. The contrast seems to be between
type and individual. If philosophy and
poetry differ, how can the difference be
characterized? Sometimes it seems to dis-
appear altogether. "And a man who is
puzzled and wonders thinks himself ig-
norant (whence even the lover of myth is
in a sense a lover of wisdom, for the myth
is composed of wonders)." (*Metaphysics*,
982b18) What we might expect to find
here is that philosophy and poetry in their
different ways provide accounts which dis-
solve wonder. But this is not what the pas-
sage says. The myth is not said to assuage
wonder but to be composed of wonders.
The *philosophos* begins with wonder and
replaces it with an account; the *philomy-
thos* loves an accumulation of wonders.
This is most suggestive. The *terminus ad
quem* of the lover of myth is the *terminus
a quo* of the lover of wisdom. Nonetheless,
we should remember that philosophy is
fulfilled in contemplative awe.

If we turn now to a passage in which
Aristotle criticizes Plato, another element
is added. "But further all things cannot
come from the forms in any of the usual

senses of 'from.' And to say that they are patterns and the other things share in them is to use empty words and poetical metaphors." (999a19 ff.) In Book Beta of the *Metaphysics,* Aristotle lists among the problems or aporiai of the science he is seeking this: Are the principles of perishable and imperishable things the same? Notice the way in which he refers to some of his predecessors.

> The school of Hesiod and all the theologians thought only of what was plausible to themselves, and had no regard to us. For, asserting the first principles to be gods and born of gods, they say that the things which did not taste of nectar and ambrosia became mortal; and clearly they are using words which are familiar to themselves, yet what they have said about the very application of these causes is above our comprehension. For if the gods taste of nectar and ambrosia for their pleasure, these are in no wise the causes of their existence; and if they taste them to maintain their existence, how can gods who need food be eternal?—But into the subtleties of the mythologists it is not worth our while to inquire seriously; those, however, who use the language of proof we must cross-examine . . . (1000a9 ff.)

Theological poets, who speak mythically, are contrasted with philosophers who speak apodictically. The matter remains subtle, however, since Aristotle goes on to quote some *verses* of Empedocles whom he does not number among the theological poets.

We now have an adverbial characterization of the discourse of the philosopher and we can identify the non-philosopher as one who does not speak apodictically. Can we replace these negations? The non-philosopher is the poet and his language is metaphorical. Here we have an Aristotelian expression of the ancient quarrel of which Plato spoke. You might rightly wonder—being philosophers all—how I managed to move so easily between myth and metaphor, conflating the two as I have done. The theological poets are said to express themselves mythically and the mark of poetic expression is metaphor. That is how I make the connection.

If we were to consult the *Index Aristotelicus* of Bonitz for occurrences of *mythos,* we would find ourselves referred mainly to the *Poetics.* The term is translated as plot and this is a new and quasi-technical use of it.[3] The plot is the logic of the events depicted on the tragic stage, the σύστασις τῶν πραγμάτων,[4] and it is a subtle blend of show and tell. Myth in the sense of plot is not verbal; it is only when Aristotle speaks of diction, the speeches of the characters, that the problem of metaphor is raised. The plot, the mythos, is a logos (1460a27-8), the intelligible structure of the events. If the term "myth" is used in a new way in the *Poetics*, the old meaning is also there, as when Aristotle says that the tragic poet takes the old *mythoi* and imposes a *mythos* on them. (1451b24) Why is it important to note this?

We have seen Aristotle refer to the theological poets as precursors of philosophy and give us an adverbial expression of their difference from the philosopher. What the adverb modifies is an accounting, discoursing. Is there a counterpart, in this stage antecedent to philosophy, to the logic of action which is the tragic plot and to the metaphor which is a feature of its diction? The tragedy cannot be equated with what is said; rather there is an enact-

ment, an imitation of *praxis* (1450a3-4),
which includes among other things
speeches employing metaphor. That is
precisely the difference between narrative
poetry and dramatic imitation. We have
been taught to think that there is some-
thing ritualistic and dramatic which pre-
ceded the accounts of the theological
poets. Gilbert Murray's suggestion that
tragedy has its ultimate origin in the
Molpe, which includes a mimesis, a dra-
matic imitation, as well as the telling of a
tale, provides us what we want.[5] The
Molpe can be considered a ritualistic song-
and-dance performance. Thus, myths in
the usual sense involve a doing as well as
a saying, and that is also true of myth in
the technical sense of the *Poetics*.

The upshot of these considerations is
that the myth which preceded philosophy
and in some sense is superseded by it,
while its language is characterized as
metaphorical, is not to be identified with
the myth and metaphor which are achieve-
ments of a conscious kind and which are
contemporaneous with philosophy. This
means that the one contrast will not wholly

do for the other; the distinction between philosophy and preceding myths is not the same as the distinction between philosophy and poetry.

A word about antecedent myths. Schelling has taught us[6] to classify views on myth under three headings: (1) myths taken as first steps towards a scientific explanation; (2) myths taken as deliberate allegories which must be interpreted to get at their literal truth; (3) myths taken to have their own truth which is irreducible to that of science. One of the fascinating things about Aristotle is that we can see him embracing at different times each of these three views on myth. Passages we have already looked at, where philosophy is seen as a replacement of myth, exemplify the first view. The second view is present when he entertains the view that history is cyclic. In the past philosophy flourished and myths are a popular expression of austere philosophical truth.[7] Given that, when philosophy has fallen into dissuetude and only the myths remain, we can probe them for the literal truths they encode. Finally, in the *Poetics*,[8]

discussing the truth of poetry, Aristotle
can be seen to take some version of the
third view.

If we now return to the adverbial con-
trast of philosophy and theological poetry
and ask after the provenance of "apodic-
tically," a quite definite conception of
philosophical discourse emerges from the
fact that it is in the *Posterior Analytics*
that Aristotle provides us with an analysis
of apodictic discourse. Apodictic discourse
is nothing other than the demonstrative
syllogism. If "apodictic" modifies syllo-
gism, there are other modifiers as well.
If some discourse is apodictic, other is
dialectical or probable, yet other rhetori-
cal or persuasive. Some discourse is only
seemingly sound and it is noteworthy
that one way the syllogism can fail to
be valid is when one of its terms is
used metaphorically.[9] Whence emerges a
stern picture, a cascade, a declension from
the most effective kind of discourse. Dia-
lectical discourse is less than apodictic and
rhetorical discourse is lesser still. Sophisti-
cal discourse simply drops off the scale
and so too, it would seem, does poetic

discourse which is characterized by metaphor.

It may well be asked if this negative attitude adequately sums up Aristotle's appraisal of poetry. Were this all he had to say on the subject, it would be curious that the *Poetics* ever got written or, if written, why it does not seem to be more like the *Sophistical Refutations*. I will not pursue the matter now because I want to draw attention to the austere conception of philosophical discourse the negative attitude seems to invite.

Aristotle's reader will not long wonder where he might go to find the sort of apodictic discourse that is ranked above the discourse of the theological poets. He has it right before his eyes, an Aristotelian treatise. Nonetheless, given the analysis of the apodictic in the *Posterior Analytics*, he may be puzzled. Developed with a keen eye on what, a century later, would be codified in Euclid's *Elements*, the *Posterior Analytics* present a view of *episteme* which seems seldom exemplified by the Aristotelian treatises, certainly only most imperfectly exemplified by them.

This has led, you will know, to studies
which ask what Aristotle's actual method
was, as opposed to the ideal sketched in
the *Posterior Analytics*.[10] And he will find
in the treatises clues to the discrepancy.
It is the mark of the wise man to ask for
only as much precision as the subject mat-
ter allows. (1094b12) Disciplines can be
ranked in several ways, either by method
or by the dignity of the subject matter.
(*De anima*, 402a) Discourse about the
highest things is dissatisfying from the
point of view of strict scientific rigor, but
it is nonetheless most desirable because of
the eminence of its objects.

But such clues aggravate rather than
alleviate the problem. We are still con-
fronted with a methodological cadenza, a
falling away from the rigor Aristotle seems
to want to attribute to philosophical dis-
course. However difficult it may be to re-
alize that rigor, Aristotle has, perhaps
malgré lui, bequeathed us an ideal of
philosophical discourse which ill accords
with the actual history of the discipline.
If we needed a single couplet to express
the way in which philosophical language,

austerely understood, differs from poetic language, the obvious candidate would be literal/metaphorical. And the tough-minded philosopher has little difficulty in knowing what to make of metaphorical language. It is meaningless. Thus spake any number of philosophers not so many decades ago and it was not only poetry proper—or improper—that fell on the other side of meaningfulness. The tribe of which I speak was practising a discipline which oddly had no history. It was always just coming into existence with the development of a new litmus test which, applied to historical philosophers, found them wanting in the extreme. Metaphysics and ethics were cast along with poetry into that outer darkness where there is metaphorical weeping and gnashing of teeth. Such an attitude begets a fairly univocal notion of the appropriate style of philosophy.

Not that we need to turn to such iconoclasts of unlamented memory in order to find the thin conception of philosophy and its appropriate style. A bald and barefoot statement of the conception is this: Philosophy inhabits an island of rational discourse lapped on its eastern shores by the dark irrational tides of primitive ritual and myth. Out of this unpromising scum—no wonder Thales was enamored of water as the principle of all things—philosophy scuttled ashore and swiftly learned to speak in those dulcet and intellectually satisfying tones we all know and love so well. This achievement is threatened by a willed plunge into the irrational. Looking westward, philosophy, like stout Cortez, surveys the unsettling seas of poetry, of drama, of metaphorical discourse. The philosopher must ever be on his guard against his putative fellows who would cry out with Leopardi

> Il naufragar m'è dolce in questo mare:
> To sink in such a sea were sweet to me.

Are we not all, to some degree, in the grips of that very narrow conception of the nature of philosophical discourse? When we think of a piece of philosophy, we are likely to think of an article in *The Review of Metaphysics, Mind, The Philosophical Review* or, if we have been well brought up, *The New Scholasticism.* As

for longer examples, we would imagine a
book the chapters of which look pretty
much like articles of the kind just men-
tioned. Well, I have already disclosed the
sordid secret that the first philosophers
wrote in verse. This may not disturb our
sense that we now know a piece of philo-
sophical discourse when we see it and that
having regular lines that rhyme would be
a sufficient sign that the discourse we are
confronted with is not philosophical. That
is, we may feel, philosophy has long since
outgrown its original confusion of literary
genres. But has it?

I owe to Julian Marias, in his *Philosophy
as Dramatic Theory*,[11] the reminder that
philosophy has made use, over the cen-
turies, of the following genres: poetry,
aphorisms, dialogues, lecture notes, com-
mentaries, meditations, autobiography,
treatises, essays, prayers, fragments and
pensées, disputed questions, *summae*, on
and on. With this reminder before us,
would we still want to say—taking into
account Nietzsche, Kierkegaard, Wittgen-
stein and Heidegger—that philosophy has
at last evolved beyond a variety of genres

and learned to settle for a single recognizable one? I think not. Consequently, if we wish to examine the difference between philosophical and poetical discourse, with an eye to saying something about philosophical style, we must from the beginning eschew a simplistic notion of the kind of discourse philosophy is.

2. *Iuxta mentem divi Thomae*

If we can believe Curtius, the ancient quarrel lay dormant thoughout the early Middle Ages until it flared up again with St. Thomas Aquinas. Referring to Thomas's theory of knowledge and art, he writes, "Behind this opposition, to be sure, there lies the eternal quarrel between the philosopher and the poet. Thomism made the quarrel flare up anew."[12] Now, it can be taken as a maxim that, when Curtius is sure, wise men doubt. What is the basis for his judgment?

But the *artes*, in which Thierry of Chartres still saw the sum of philosophy, had now to resign any such claim. Their framework had become too narrow for the enlarged realm of

profane disciplines. Thomas Aquinas' dictum,
'septem artes liberales non sufficienter dividunt
philosophiam theoricam,' announces a new
era.[13]

Elsewhere,[14] it is clear that Curtius takes
this statement to put an end to the con-
fusion of philosophy and poetry. "The old
connection between *artes* and philosophy
is severed at a blow."

This is an odd interpretation. It is true
that prior to the introduction of the com-
plete *corpus Aristotelicum* toward the end
of the Twelfth Century, there were many
who took the liberal arts, the trivium and
quadrivium, to be identical with secular
learning and to constitute the sufficient
propaideutic for the study of Holy Scrip-
ture. If secular learning is identical with
philosophy and if philosophy is identical
with the liberal arts, then there is indeed
an identification of secular learning and
the arts. But to call this an identification of
philosophy and *poetry* would be a strange
simplification. After all, numbered among
the liberal arts are arithmetic, geometry
and astronomy. What the context of
the Thomistic passage quoted by Curtius

makes clear—and it is not without significance that Curtius quotes it at second hand[15]—is that the liberal arts tradition is deftly subsumed within the wider Aristotelian conception of philosophy.

Having divided philosophy into theoretical and practical, Aristotle goes on to enumerate three theoretical sciences, natural philosophy, mathematics and theology, and three practical sciences, ethics, economics and politics.[16] No mention of poetry.[17] Does that mean philosophy is thereby distinguished from all arts, including poetry? Not at all. The arts of the trivium are reduced to logic and the arts of the quadrivium to mathematics and thus the liberal arts make up the first two stages in that order of learning which, as we mentioned earlier, Thomas gleaned from Aristotle.[18] Poetry is found in the liberal arts as an aspect of grammar. Whatever St. Thomas's views on the relationship between philosophy and poetry, they can scarcely be found in the passage cited by Curtius.

Later, in discussing Albertino Mussato, Curtius states the matter in a way inconsistent with his other remarks, those just mentioned. "It is clear that the Dominican [Mussato] is not concerned with 'attacking' or 'belittling' poetry, but with assigning it a place in the system of disciplines which Thomas had firmly established. The crucial point of the discussion is the question of the nature of the metaphors found in the Bible."[19] Here we have a more accurate portrayal of Thomas's position. Poetry is not so much distinguished from philosophy as it forms part of the network of disciplines which can be brought together under that commodious term. He who pursues wisdom, it seems, must concern himself with poetry as a discipline required for the *esse* or *bene esse* of wisdom. This is what we must now examine.

a) *The Least of Doctrines*

We have seen that "apodictic" modifies the discourse or syllogism Aristotle apparently takes to be characteristic of philosophy, whereas "metaphorical" modifies mythic and poetic discourse. Since apodictic reasoning is the subject matter of the

Posterior Analytics, we are not surprised
to find Thomas, in his proemium to his
commentary on that work, develop a hi-
erarchy of discourse.

"Man lives by art and reasoning,"
Thomas quotes, and by this is set off from
other animals. The latter live by natural
instinct and are as it were acted on rather
than act, whereas man is directed in his
actions by the judgment of his own reason.
The various arts have been devised by
man in order that he might proceed easily
and in an orderly fashion. Whence comes
the definition of art as "certa ordinatio
rationis quomodo per determinata media
ad debitum finem actus humani perveni-
ant: the fixed orientation of reason thanks
to which human acts attain their fitting
end in a determinate way."[20]

What is obvious from this opening of
the proemium of the commentary is that
"art" is being used to cover the whole
range of disciplines. Not operative yet is
the distinction elsewhere made between
science and art; then art will be restricted
to the status of a virtue of practical rea-
soning.[21] The common use of the term is

already required for an understanding of the phrase "liberal arts." A fortiori it is needed when "art" ranges over all disciplines.[22] Any reader of Aquinas is familiar with his habit of using terms in a common and proper sense. *Abstractio* is sometimes distinguished from *separatio,* when the two terms are used in a narrow or proper sense; used commonly *abstractio* embraces *separatio* and a*bstractio* (in the narrow sense). So too *separatio* sometimes includes *abstractio* and *separatio* (in the narrow sense).[23] If the terms in question had but one sense, we would be confronted with the crudest confusion. In much the same way, the common meaning of "art" is not operative when art is distinguished from science.

In the text we are examining, Thomas is of course concerned with logic, the art directive of the very act of reason itself. Manual skill involves reason's direction of bodily movements; logic is reason's directing of reasoning itself. This is why logic is called the *ars artium.*[24] Logic, in turn, will be subdivided if there are different rational acts to be directed. Thus, the logical art of defining, and attendant arts, bear on *intelligentia indivisibilium sive incomplexorum,* what has traditionally been called simple apprehension. A second act of reason, composition and division, calls for the logic of propositions. The third act directed by logic is discourse.[25]

The maxim that art imitates nature is invoked to establish that artful or rational acts mimick, to the degree this is possible, natural activities. But the latter are of three major kinds. Sometimes nature acts with necessity and cannot fail, whereas at other times nature acts in such a way that frequently or for the most part its ends are achieved. And, of course, it follows from this that sometimes nature fails.

> These three are also found in acts of reason. There is a certain process of reason involving necessity, in which the lack of truth is impossible: it is through this process of reason that the certitude of science is achieved. There is another process of reason in which truth is arrived at by and large but necessity is not had. A third process of reason is such that reason fails to arrive at truth because of a defect in its starting point. . . .[26]

Thomas can now link these distinctions to syllogism and identify the works of Aristotle's Organon which treat the special art in question. In what he calls judicative logic, reasoning resolves a judgment into principles with certainty and this either because of the form of reasoning as such, thanks to the shape of the syllogism, something discussed in the *Prior Analytics*, or because of the matter, the kind of principles to which resolution is made, namely those which are per se and necessary. This point is often made by distinguishing necessity of consequences from the necessity of the consequent.[27]

There is also a logic of discovery which does not always involve necessity. The notion of types of discourse falling away from apodictic or necessary discourse having been introduced, Thomas spells out the declension of modes we talked about earlier. "In processu rationis, qui non est cum omnimoda certitudine, gradus aliquis invenitur, secundum quod magis vel minus ad perfectam certitudinem acceditur: a hierarchy can be discerned in that process of reasoning in which there is not perfect certitude insofar as it attains more or less closely to certitude."[28] It is on the bottom rung of this hierarchy that we find poetic argumentation.

Dialectical or probable argument is productive of opinion and the logical art concerned with it is developed in the *Topics* of Aristotle. Rhetorical argument is productive of *suspicio*, perhaps renderable as surmise, and is dealt with, needless to say, in Aristotle's *Rhetoric*. What is opined or surmised? The object of knowledge, opinion or surmise is, as Thomas puts, one side of a contradiction. That is, what is to be determined by these processes of reason can be formally expressed as "p v -p?" The apodictic or demonstrative syllogism enables one to conclude that p is necessarily true and -p necessarily false. It is that exclusion of the contradictory of what one holds to be true that is only imperfectly present in dialectical and rhetorical discourse. How does poetry fit into this scheme?

> Sometimes thought inclines to one side of a
> contradiction on account of a representation,

in the way in which a man may abominate
food if it is distastefully represented to him.
The *Poetics* is concerned with this sort of
thing since the poet commends the virtuous
by means of a fitting representation.[29]

This is, you will agree, a surprising pas-
sage. While it may be attractive in the
way in which it links poetry with other
modes of discourse, providing us with a
sense of "poetic argumentation," it makes
of poetry a *pis aller* of an apparently ex-
pendable sort. Surely arguments of an-
other kind can be fashioned on behalf of
the desirability of virtue over vice. Poetry
thus seems merely a way of doing some-
thing that can be better done otherwise.
Furthermore, the overtly moral purpose
of poetry that Thomas stresses leaves a
great deal to be desired. It would be easy
to go on a bit about the diminished view
of poetry Thomas has here—and I shall do
so in a moment—but we must not leave
this passage without drawing attention to
something of importance.

In the movement—downward—from di-
alectical to rhetorical discourse, we might
want to make explicit what Thomas leaves

implicit, namely that rhetorical persuasion
does not address pure intellect but ap-
peals to the emotions as well. The further
move to poetry might then be taken to
carry this more than intellectual appeal
along with it, the representation of which
Thomas speaks eliciting a response not
narrowly rational though not thereby ir-
rational or "emotive." It is here we can
see, I think, the genesis of Maritain's ex-
tension of St. Thomas's notion of the judg-
ment by connaturality or inclination to
poetic knowledge.[30] Let us return now to
the base place to which Thomas has rele-
gated poetry.

As it happens, texts which assert the
diminished conception of poetry occur
precisely where St. Thomas is intent on
overcoming it. For example, in the pro-
logue to his *Scriptum super libros Senten-
tiarum,* when he asks if the mode of Scrip-
ture should be *artificialis,* he entertains
this objection:

> The same mode should not be common to
> sciences which differ maximally. But the poetic
> [mode], which contains the least truth, differs
> maximally from that of this science which is

most true. Therefore, since the former makes use of metaphorical locutions, the mode of this science ought not be the same.[31]

The objection captures nicely the notion of poetry and metaphor Thomas embraced when commenting on the *Posterior Analytics* and we can see why, confronted with the undeniably metaphorical nature of so many Scriptural passages, that notion should cause him trouble. Notice first of all his direct response to the objection.

Poetic knowledge is concerned with things which because of their defect of truth cannot be grasped by intellect; that is why reason must be seduced by means of similitudes. Theology, on the other hand, deals with things above reason and that is why the symbolic mode is common to them both since neither is proportioned to reason.[32]

This is not a defense of poetry that would commend itself to Shelly or perhaps to many others; yet something suggested in the Aristotelian commentary is absent from it, namely, that poetry does in one way what could be done better in another. Here poetic language is necessi-

tated by the want of truth in the things
talked about, the want of determination
or necessity or fixity in its subject matter.
Accordingly, when God, who exceeds our
capacity to understand, is the subject, a
similar deficiency is felt and recourse is
had to metaphor.[33]

The parallel discussion in the *Summa
theologiae* puts the contrast somewhat dif-
ferently. "The poet uses metaphors for the
sake of representation because a repre-
sentation is naturally delightful to men,
but Sacred Scripture employs metaphors
out of necessity and utility."[34] The objec-
tion to which this is a response has de-
scribed poetry as *infima inter omnes doc-
trinas,* the least of doctrines. The *Sed
contra* gives us a kind of definition of
metaphor. "Tradere autem aliquid sub
similitudine est metaphoricum: metaphor
treats of a thing through a likeness of it."
When we consider the reason St. Thomas
gives for the need of metaphor in speaking
of God a serious difficulty arises. The prin-
ciple he invokes for this necessity would
appear to entail that all talk about God is

metaphorical. That, as you will know, is not a conclusion Thomas could accept.

b) *Metaphor and Analogy*

We have seen a number of passages in which St. Thomas says some rather slighting things about poetic language and the put-down does not seem to be put aside when he justifies the use of metaphorical and symbolic language in Scripture. The elements of this justification can easily appear to call into question talk about God which aspires to be other than metaphorical, whether such talk occurs in natural or supernatural theology. This is something which must interest any effort to discover the nature of the distinction between poetry and philosophy.

The hierarchy of discourse provides us with a way of distinguishing philosophy from poetry if the former makes use of the apodictic and the latter makes use of the metaphorical or symbolic mode. But a moment's reflection makes it clear that we cannot rest with such a simplistic solution. When St. Thomas compares philosophical

disciplines, he says that this can be done
in two ways, either with reference to their
objects or their modes. On the basis of
modes, mathematics is going to come out
far ahead of both moral philosophy and
metaphysics. On the basis of objects, meta-
physics is going to rank higher than any
of the others.[35] Now "metaphysics" is the
term we use to designate the treatise in
which Aristotle is concerned with the cul-
minating goal of philosophy, wisdom: such
knowledge as men can achieve of the di-
vine. Theology, discourse about God, is
the telos towards which the whole philo-
sophical enterprise tends. Consequently,
if all talk about God is metaphorical, and
if metaphor is the mark of poetic discourse,
the very foundation of a distinction be-
tween philosophy and poetry is in jeop-
ardy. Clearly this is not a matter we could
pass over undiscussed.

Consider now the following argument
St. Thomas fashions in discussing the
prevalence of metaphors in Scripture.

It is fitting that Sacred Scripture should treat
divine and spiritual things under the likeness

of the corporeal. God provides for all things in a manner befitting their natures. But it is natural to man that he should come to intelligible things by way of the sensible, because all our knowledge takes its rise from sensation. Hence in Sacred Scripture spiritual things are fittingly presented to us by way of bodily metaphors.[36]

The key to the argument is the claim that our knowledge begins with sensible things; they are what we first know and talk about. Knowledge of them provides us with a basis for knowing suprasensible things, divine and spiritual things, and we transfer the terms used to speak of sensible things to spiritual things. Nothing will be more familiar to the student of St. Thomas than this claim but, in this context, it has a surprising implication. The context is a justification of bodily metaphors in speaking of spiritual things. The question is: How can we possibly speak of them otherwise than metaphorically?

The question can be answered and the difficulty resolved only if the principle here invoked can accommodate the claim that sometimes the transfer of terms from

sensible to spiritual things does not involve
metaphor. We do not find in St. Thomas
any suggestion that we have a special
spiritual vocabulary. The terms that make
up the language of theology are always
terms which have a prior use to speak of
ordinary physical things. Our knowledge
of God is gained from knowledge of crea-
tures. But the way in which we name or
talk about things reflects the way we know
them. Thus God is always denominated
from creatures and talked about with
reference to them.[37] Metaphor thus seems
to be an ineluctable mark of theological
discourse.

The difficulty before us directs us to pas-
sages in Thomas where we are most likely
to find him saying things about our sub-
ject. Needless to say, St. Thomas wrote no
treatise on poetic discourse or on meta-
phor; for that matter, he wrote no formal
work on language as such. We will find his
views on these topics embedded in discus-
sions of various problems, not quite *obiter
dicta,* but nonetheless rather strictly con-
fined to the narrow issue before him. A
Thomistic theory of poetry is necessarily

a posthumously constructed one, built up
from hints and inchoative asides. On the
difference between metaphorical and non-
metaphorical discourse, we find such help
as we do mainly in discussions of talk
about God.

There is little doubt that the most in-
fluential work on a significant aspect of
St. Thomas's theory of language is the
opusculum *De nominum analogia* written
by Cardinal Cajetan during the summer
vacation of 1498.[38] Basing himself on a text
to be found in St. Thomas's commentary
on the *Sentences,* Cajetan distinguished
three kinds of analogous term: analogy of
inequality, analogy of attribution, and
analogy of proportionality. The third kind
of analogy is further distinguished into
analogy of proper proportionality and
analogy of improper proportionality, that
is, metaphor. Some of you will know that
I have been a critic of this portion of the
teaching of the great commentator on the
Summa theologiae. It is precisely in his
commentary on *Ia,* q. 16, a. 6, a parallel
text to that from the *Sentences* which pro-
vides the structure of Cajetan's opuscu-

lum, that one sees how unsure a guide in
these matters the cardinal is. In the *Summa
theologiae,* St. Thomas wrote this: "Sed
quando aliquid dicitur analogice de multis,
illud invenitur secundum propriam ration-
em in uno eorum tantum, a quo alia de-
nominantur: when something is said anal-
ogously of many it is found according to
its proper notion in one of them alone from
which the others are denominated."[39] This
is a remark of quite general scope. Un-
fortunately, not only is Cajetan unable to
accept it as the definition of the analogous
term, he suggests that it is better thought
of as inapplicable to a truly analogous
term![40] Cajetan had written his little work
on analogous names prior to commenting
on the *Summa theologiae* and his own
theory has a way of getting between him
and the text of St. Thomas.

This is not the time for me to rehearse
arguments I have developed at length
elsewhere.[41] For now I wish only to draw
attention to the way in which Cajetan links
metaphor and analogy while wishing to
distinguish the two. This is exactly what
we find in St. Thomas. In his treatise on

the divine names, Thomas asks if any term
is properly said of God,[42] and the dis-
cussion makes it clear that he is asking
whether any term is said of God other
than metaphorically. We have already
seen why this must be a problem for him.
If the human mind is such that it must
derive knowledge of God from knowledge
of creatures, and if our language reflects
the trajectory of our knowing, then all
terms applied to God will be drawn from
talk about creatures. But to speak of some-
thing in terms appropriate to something
else is to speak metaphorically of it. This
and other objections set the stage for the
discussion whose thesis is, "Non igitur
omnia nomina dicuntur de Deo meta-
phorice, sed aliqua dicuntur proprie: not
all names are said of God metaphorically,
but some are said properly."[43]

What is needed is a criterion for dis-
tinguishing proper from improper predi-
cation or naming. We know God from the
perfections in creatures which proceed
from Him, perfections which exist in God
in a more eminent way than they do in
creatures. Our intellect grasps them in

their creaturely mode and that is how our
terms signify them. Two aspects of the
names attributed to God must therefore be
considered: the perfection signified and
the way of signifying it. If we attend to
the perfection signified and not to the
creaturely mode embedded in the signi-
fication, some names can be said properly
of God and indeed more properly of Him
than of creatures.[44] "Quantum ad modum
significandi, omne nomen cum defectu
est."[45]

Why is it that only some and not all
words signifying perfections can be attrib-
uted to God so long as we prescind from
the creaturely mode of having the perfec-
tion? Surely all created perfections pro-
ceed from God as cause, and effects are
said by Thomas to be like their causes.
The answer is that there are some perfec-
tions which are proper to creatures as such
and not simply in the way the creature has
them. It is one thing to speak of words
like "being," "good," "wise" and "just" and
quite another to speak of "stone" and "fire"
and "lion." Existence and goodness are
found in limited ways in creatures and this

is reflected in the meanings of "being" and "good." Leoninity is as such a limited perfection. To say that God possesses or is it in an unlimited fashion would be to speak of God inappropriately, as corporeal.[46] The criterion we seek, put in Thomas's quasi-technical vocabulary is this: when the *res significata* does not include limitations, though the *modus significandi* does, the word can be said properly of God; when the *res significata* includes limitations, the word can be said of God only metaphorically.[47]

Was Cajetan wrong to suggest that the metaphor is a kind of analogous term? If "properly" is attached to analogy and "improperly" to metaphor, then metaphor is distinct from and not a type of analogous term. Nonetheless, as I have argued elsewhere, St. Thomas uses both "metaphor" and "analogy" in wide as well as restricted senses.[48] It is in their restricted or narrow senses that they are distinguished from one another; in its wide sense we are justified in taking metaphor as embracing metaphor and analogy, in their narrow senses, and analogy, in the wide sense, as

embracing metaphor and analogy, in their
narrow senses. Far from jeopardizing the
clarity of the distinction between meta-
phor and analogy, these precisions are a
condition of its intelligibility.

Such discussions enable us to generalize
about metaphorical talk. When a man is
called a lion, the intent is not to say that
he is another instance of the type, though
that is intended when he is called an ani-
mal. We cannot find in the meaning of
"lion" the reason for calling a man one.
Where then is the reason to be found? St.
Thomas's suggestion is that the similarity
is neither univocal nor analogical, both
of which depend upon meanings. Rather
the metaphorical extension of a term is
grounded in something associated with the
things of which the term is properly predi-
cated. It is because of his roaring or his
courage, traits associated wtih lions though
not part of the meaning of "lion," that
Richard is called a lion.[4]

We have then the solution we sought.
Although in explaining metaphor St.
Thomas invokes our mode of knowing
God, which goes from creatures to God

and involves the extension to Him of terms first fashioned to speak of creatures, not every such extension is merely metaphorical. This enables us to avoid saying that the language of metaphysics and of theology is poetic. Nonetheless, as we have seen, it does not enable us to say that such language is apodictic. And that, as the sequel will show, has important consequences for our view of philosophical style.

3. *Three Spectra of Discourse*

We have seen St. Thomas develop from Aristotelian sources a hierarchy of modes of discourse based on types of argument. There is argument in the strict sense which concludes with necessity some necessary truth; that was the meaning of apodictic discourse. There is argument which provides grounds for holding something to be true without enabling us wholly to exclude its contradictory; this was the meaning of dialectical discourse. There is argument less rigorous still which provides both intellectual and appetitive grounds for holding something to be true; this is rhetorical or persuasive discourse. Finally, poetic discourse is taken to be a kind of argument which by means of representations induces us to accept something because it is pleasing. *Id quod visum placet.*

If discourse can be ranged on a scale or spectrum in terms of types of argument, another spectrum could be established in terms of the musical aspect of language. One way of comparing poetic language with philosophical language is to say that the latter addresses itself directly to understanding, whereas the former works not only with the meanings of words, but also, perhaps chiefly, with the musical aspects of the vehicle of meaning, articulated sound.[50] This point was made to excess by the Symbolists when they held that the essential effect of poetic language can be achieved with nonsense syllables. There is, of course, something to be said for this. T. S. Eliot tells of his initial appreciation of Dante when, knowing only how to pronounce Italian, he savored the music of the *Divina Commedia* without being able to understand what he was reading. Hugh

Kenner, in *The Pound Era,* has similarly argued that the poetic effect is essentially detachable from cognitive meaning.[51]

Imagine a scale at one end of which there are only modulated sounds: humming, perhaps tra la la, where our attention is directed to pitch and rhythm alone, to ordered measured sound. The basic vehicle of language is musical in this way, and the music does not stop when meaning is added to it.[52] At the other end of the scale, we can imagine language so used as to diminish or conceal its musical side. In between would fall those uses of language in which theatrical and rhetorical and forensic effects are achieved by artful employment of the music of language. In poetry, with its measured lines, its alliteration, its rhymes which organize and group units of meaningful sound, we would have a perfect vocal music to enhance and supplement and in some cases to supplant cognitive meaning. Notice that, since there can be no language without music—sound as vehicle, sense as tenor—the language of philosophy is not and cannot be artless; it can only be good

or bad art. It could be argued that the
rhetoric of philosophical language is a con-
summate art—if the best art is that which
conceals itself. Like the music of the
spheres, the philosophical use of language
might be seen as striving to make the ve-
hicle of its sense inaudible. I shall return
to this.

Far more than the meanings of words
must be understood if we are to under-
stand what another says. The contem-
porary notion of a speech-act rings the
changes on this truth.[53] What we do when
we speak is not exhausted by what the
words or sentences we say mean: we as-
sert, we reply, we refer to objects, we
make a promise. In J. L. Austin's phrase,
we *do* things *with* words. The things we
say are part of a vast network which must
be known by those who would understand
us. A sentence does not *express* how it is
to be understood. That is why to know a
language is to know so much more than
what the words and sentences mean. This
seems to be part of what Wittgenstein was
getting at with the concept of a language-
game.

The speech-acts in which some pieces of discourse are embedded may seem so simple as to be transparent or even absent. Thus, if the philosopher's use of language is typically to explain and argue and to make clear the way things are, then the fact that his words refer as well as mean or state answers to presumed questions may seem presuppositions so stable and obvious as to be beneath notice. We might even—wrongly—think that this is a feature of discourse in which indicative sentences predominate. It is when we are saying something which has the effect of promising, marrying, cursing, praying, beseeching, consecrating bread and wine, inducing awe in our listener, on and on, that we are more likely to be aware of the drama which sustains performative utterances and thanks to which the spoken effects the illocutionary act it does.[54]

There have not been wanting philosophers who thought that indicative sentences whose truth or falsity seems easily settled—"the cat is on the mat" is a favored example—are the standard use of language, since such language *seems* to require very little attention to a dramatic setting to catch its point. Mention of that dramatic setting as a vehicle of which meaning in the narrow sense is the tenor may seem superfluous, even an affectation. This supposedly standard use of language might be better regarded as an achievement and a luxury.

I think of the great opening chapter of the *Metaphysics* where Aristotle puts before our eyes the panorama of human rational activity. He pictures man as immersed in the world and first overcoming his ontological isolation by means of perception in a decidedly practical setting: the beast's concern for survival, for food, for sex. That beast survives in our own perception, but we can, beyond looking-out-for, also just look. This is an adumbration of *theoria*. Aristotle moves on, from outer to inner sense, from experience to art, the emphasis remaining on the practical which is accorded chronological (and thus linguistic) primacy. *Theoria,* like play, requires leisure and can only come when concern for the next meal and whether we will have one is no longer a matter of constant concern. In this perspective, making utterances like "The cat is on the mat" could function as a triumphant and reassuring remark. Or one of warning. The beast is back. If Tarzan says it to Jane, it may be in a husky warning whisper. Decadents like ourselves might utter it to illustrate internal rhyme or iambic trimeter. What "The cat is on the mat" *means* does not decide what we are *doing* when we say it. What does decide? The context. The understood context.

Considerations such as these must affect the way in which we speak of philosophical discourse. If we take the first spectrum, the ranging of discourse in terms of types of argument, it turns out to be impossible to think of philosophical discourse as an unalleviated suite of apodictic utterances, of demonstrative syllogisms, as if philosophy amounted to nothing more than assigning values to the variables in a formal system. For one thing, as Aristotle observed, dialectic is indispensable to all disciplines.[55] This being the case, we expect to find dialectical considerations permeating any philosophical effort. Added to this

is the fact that rigor is a function of sub-
ject matter. It is a mark of the wise man
to demand only as much precision as the
subject matter allows. We have already
indicated how this affects our expectations
of metaphysics. An equally striking loose-
ness is to be found in practical philosophy
because of the contingency and variability
of its subject matter.[56] In short, the first
spectrum having to do with types of argu-
ment does not provide us with any single
measure of the appropriate style of philo-
sophical discourse.

Earlier I mentioned the variety of gen-
res in which philosophers have expressed,
and continue to express, their thought.
How is it that Thales and Heraclitus and
Plato and Aristotle and Marcus Aurelius
and Boethius and Anselm and Hume and
Nietzsche and Heidegger can be found
classified in the same section of our li-
braries and anthologized in books which
introduce beginners to philosophy? And
what is one to make of a Kierkegaard who
employed as well as discussed something
he called indirect communication? One
who has a univocal and narrow concep-

tion of philosophy will have a correspond-
ingly exiguous notion of philosophical dis-
course. He may be inclined to dismiss the
majority of philosophers as simply not
making the grade. Someone like Kierke-
gaard might be dismissed with the obser-
vation that he is out to change our lives,
not merely to change our minds with an
argument. But when did philosophy cease
to be an effort to become a certain sort of
person?

St. Thomas accepts the classical view of
philosophy which saw it as a cluster of
disciplines and activities teleologically or-
dered to the acquisition of wisdom de-
scribed as such knowledge as men can
attain of the divine. This telos is the hu-
man good and it cannot be separated from
either moral philosophy or its culmination
in contemplation. Surely if we ask what
the purpose of doing moral philosophy is
we must locate that purpose *extra genus
notitiae*. The reflections which make up
moral philosophy in the classical sense are
meant to affect our lives, to guide actions,
to aid in the acquisition of character. The
human good turns out to be a cluster of

virtues, practical and theoretical, the doing
well of the many modes of rational activity
of which a human is capable.

You see what I am getting at. If we
have a diminished view of what philoso-
phy is, we will have a correspondingly thin
notion of what philosophical discourse can
be. Plato's warnings about the dangers of
dialectic, in his sense of that term, have to
do with the dangerous divorce of the play
of argument from the point of seeking
arguments at all. Philosophy is not a skill
which enables us to triumph momentarily
over interlocutors. It is not the pursuit of
clarity and precision disengaged from the
uses and point of clarity and precision. It
is not a career. It is a vocation. It is the
quest for human perfection in all its ampli-
tude. St. Thomas could not, of course, be
content with the pagan conception of what
the amplitude of the human good truly is,
but that is another point. My present point
is that, with a classical conception of phil-
osophy as the pursuit of wisdom, the quest
for human perfection, we will expect and
welcome a variety of styles and literary
genres. Some styles and genres will be

more appropriate to one portion of the philosophical task than to others, but that is just what we should expect.

One of the banes of modern philosophy has been its tragic desire for a single method which would enable us to solve all philosophical problems. Such a desire has as its immediate effect the restriction of what counts as a philosophical problem. And the first casualty of it is the loss of the conception of philosophy as a way of life, as a way of becoming someone, not just an accomplished disembodied thinker, but a fulfilled human being. Its effect on the conception of what moral philosophy is and what it is out to do has been particularly unfortunate, as is being increasingly recognized by such philosophers as Iris Murdoch, Alisdair MacIntyre and G. E. M. Anscombe.[57] Practical reasoning becomes a problem or is reduced to theoretical thinking. Desire and appetite become surd elements which can ground a calculation but themselves escape appraisal. Philosophy becomes a skill instead of a concatenation of virtues.

4. *The Artful Philosopher*

If the hierarchy of arguments does not serve up the single type appropriate to philosophy, we are saved from seeing the place of poetry in that hierarchy as a dismissal of it. Metaphysics and morals are essential ingredients of philosophy and neither is noteworthy for its apodictic mode of arguing. Curtius suggested that St. Thomas did not so much mean to belittle poetry as to locate it within a far wider frame than was possible prior to the advent of the integral Aristotle in the West. When Thomas speaks of poetry he does so in terms of making, an activity of the practical intellect.[58] Poetry, as a species of art, is a species of *recta ratio factibilium:* an intellectual skill which produces artifacts, poems. The medium of poetry is language; the poem is an arrangement of words. In one of his essays, T. S. Eliot speaks of the poet at his typewriter. If you feel, as I did when I first read it, a little shiver of distaste at the phrase, perhaps this is due to our image of the poet working with a quill pen, but in any case we think of the poet fashioning on the page the artifact that is his peculiar opus. He may have composed it in his mind beforehand, more likely he falls into intermittent silences at the typewriter, he may afterward recite from memory what he has written, but it is difficult to speak of the poet at all if not as a writer. The novelist, too, and even more obviously, is a writer. Doubtless you know someone who intends to write a novel but never has; you would hesitate to call him a novelist. Is it possible that he has a novel in his head?

I now draw your attention to an astonishing fact. When philosophers speak of what philosophers do they almost never mention writing. You may think that this is because philosophers are usually teachers, but teaching too is seldom mentioned when the tasks of the philosopher are enumerated. If it were, however theoretical the activity of philosophizing is taken to be, teaching would have to be recognized, as it was by St. Thomas, as a practical activity.[59] It is an art. So too when the philosopher writes—we all do and far too much—he is practising an art. He is pro-

ducing an artifact, a piece of prose. The
activity in which he is engaged bears a
strong family resemblance to what the
poet is doing at his typewriter. Yet Brand
Blanshard's little book *On Philosophical
Style* is all but unique.[60] Why is this?

By and large, when people pursue grad-
uate studies with an eye to the Ph.D., they
study everything but teaching, despite the
fact that what they aspire to be is *doctores*,
teachers. I mean that they do not study it
formally. They do study their teachers,
witness the activity in which they are en-
gaged, and doubtless, at least in a nega-
tive way, gain a sense of how it ought to be
done. Graduate students get some train-
ing in writing. They produce an enormous
amount of papers and eventually a disser-
tation. Nonetheless, it would not be too
much to say that the concentration is al-
most exclusively on the content of these
products. The form is considered a neg-
ligible factor, or something that will sim-
ply take care of itself. Haven't they been
speaking prose all their lives? It is as if
the writing is all but inessential to what is
being done. This is false.

Try to imagine a Husserl or a Wittgenstein knowing what he thinks without writing in order to find out. The shudder felt before the image of the poet at his typewriter could be matched by picturing the philosopher at his, but in this case not because another writing instrument is envisaged as more appropriate. Yet philosophical thinking is all but inseparable from the art of writing. Sometimes, as in the cases just mentioned, the writing is not for publication. The philosopher is writing *ad seipsum;* the product is inchoative, searching, tentative. Whatever Wittgenstein's intention, most of what he wrote is finding its way into print. One half expects to see an announcement of the imminent appearance of his Baby Book. When the philosopher does write for publication, he is by definition engaged in a conscious art. In this sense, the philosopher is a poet, a maker, an artist. And, as often as not, a bad one.

Earlier considerations suggest ways in which we might describe elements of his art, but they also prevent us from developing a univocal and narrow notion of philo-

sophical style. In saying that a scale could
be developed in terms of the music of
langauge, I suggested that poetic dis-
course draws attention to the music of its
medium, of words in juxtaposition and se-
quence, so that their meanings alone can-
not account for the effect the poem has on
us. You do not need a philosopher to tell
you that this will not deliver up a single
set of criteria for a poem's being a poem.
There is an almost infinite variety among
the poems that have been made already.
Who are we to say that the future will only
reproduce the past? It is by his craft that
the poet puts the music of language to his
purposes. If the philosopher too is an artist
of language, he must be equally artful in
suiting language to his purpose. Here too,
as we have seen, it would be wrong to
think that his purpose is everywhere the
same. Is Ortega's *Meditations on Quixote*
philosophical? Is Camus's *The Myth of
Sisyphus* a philosophical work? Anyone
who insists that philosophy is always and
everywhere engaged in the pursuit of rig-
orous proof is going to have an extremely
meager philosophical library. If we take

a more commodious view and say that philosophical thinking is the amassing of considerations on behalf of a truth, we will have a way of accounting for the vast and multifarious literature which has traditionally been recognized as philosophical. We will even find ourselves constrained to admit as philosophical all sorts of writings which, usually for unexamined reasons, we had not previously thought of as philosophical. Were Chesterton and Belloc philosophers, at least sometimes? I think so. They give me reasons for thinking that something is true and they do so in ways artfully adapted to that purpose.

I have in this lecture examined the relation between philosophy and poetry with an eye to saying something about the philosophical rather than the poetic art. It may seem to you that I have brought philosophy and poetry quite close together, perhaps even too close. Often of course they are manifestly different, but sometimes the distinction blurs. Santayana once wrote a book entitled *Three Philosophical Poets*.[61] It is a book with which it is a delight to disagree and from which it is impossible not to learn. Consider the following passage from it.

> The reasonings and investigations of philosophy are arduous, and if poetry is linked with them, it can be artificially only, and with a bad grace. But the vision of philosophy is sublime. The order it reveals in the world is something beautiful, tragic, sympathetic to the mind, and just what every poet, on a small or on a large scale, is always trying to catch.[62]

The poet and the philosopher, in the practise of their respective arts, seek to give us, in their different ways, beyond and through their artifacts, a sense of the way things are. It is possible to think of them both as aiming at contemplation.

> A philosopher who attains it is, for the moment, a poet; and a poet who turns his practised and passionate imagination on the order of all things, or on anything in the light of the whole, is for that moment a philosopher.[63]

The thrill we feel in reading that sentence was intended by Santayana. It is a legitimate and integral effect of philosophical writing akin to the geometer's acronymic and triumphant Q.E.D. The philosopher ignores such aspects of his writing at his peril. Paul Claudel has a devestating essay on Descartes whom he judges to have been a bad thinker because he was a bad writer.[64] Many philosophers have triumphed over their bad prose but it is a risky gamble.

Let me conclude with a remark on the style of St. Thomas. You will know the variety of genres represented in his *Opera Omnia:* treatises, commentaries, polemical works, disputed and quodlibetal questions, letters, prayers, hymns, *summae,* compendia, biblical exegesis. Both Chenu[65] and Pieper[66] have commented on the style of St. Thomas. Pieper begins by comparing it with St. Augustine's and one fears the worst. He stresses the brilliance of style, the verbal grace, the music of Augustine's prose, its personal tone. The contrast with St. Thomas suggests itself. But listen to Pieper.

> But at bottom Thomas wishes to communicate something else entirely, and that alone; he wishes to make plain, not his own inner state, but his insight into a given subject. Such an aim does not, of course, exclude grandeur of

form; it does not exclude beauty. And that austere kind of beauty is certainly found in the writings of Thomas. There are numerous indications, moreover, that Thomas strove for such beauty.[67]

Thomas Aquinas as artist. I hope I have prepared you for that description of him. If the tribe of Thomists has served his memory poorly, some of our fault may lie in the fact that we have not imitated him in this.

NOTES

1. Victor M. Hamm, *Language, Truth and Poetry*, Marquette University Press, 1960.

2. "Et inde est quod philosophorum intentio ad hoc principaliter erat ut, per omnia quae in rebus considerabant, ad cognitionem primarum causarum pervenirent. Unde scientiam de primis causis ultimo ordinabant, cuius considerationi ultimum tempus suae vitae deputarent: primo quidem incipientes a logica quae modum scientiarum tradit, secundo procedentes ad mathematicam cuius etiam pueri possunt esse capaces, tertio ad naturalem philosophiam quae propter experientiam tempore indiget, quarto autem ad moralem philosophiam cuius iuvenis esse conveniens auditor non potest, ultimo autem scientiae divinae insistebant quae considerat primas entium causas."—*In Librum de Causis* (ed. Saffrey; Louvain, 1964), p. 2.

3. Gerald Else, *Aristotle's Poetics*, pp. 242 ff.

4. *Poetics*, 1450a15. See my "Metaphor and Fundamental Ontology," in *Studies in Analogy*, Nijhoff, 1968.

5. Gilbert Murray, *The Classical Tradition in Poetry*.

6. *Introduction à la philosophie de la mythologie*, Aubier, Paris, 1945.

7. *Metaphysics*, 995a3-6; *De coelo*, 270b5-9; 248a2-13 and *Meteor.*, 339b19-30.

8. Chapter 25. S. H. Butcher, in *Aristotle's Theory of Poetry and Fine Art* (Dover Books, 1951), devotes a chapter to Poetic Truth, pp. 163-197.

9. *Sophistical Refutations*, cap. 17.

10. M. LeBlonde, *Logique et Méthode chez Aristote*.

11. Pennsylvania State University Press, 1971, pp.

1-35; see too Richard McKeon, "Imitation and Poetry," in *Thought, Action and Passion,* University of Chicago Press, 1954, pp. 103-4.

12. Ernst Robert Curtius, *European Literature and the Latin Middle Ages,* trans. by Willard R. Trask, Princton University Press, 1953, pp. 220-1.

13. *Ibid.,* p. 57.

14. *Ibid.,* p. 213.

15. *Ibid.,* p. 57, note 65. Curtius depends on M. Grabmann, *Mitteralterliches Geistesleben,* II, (1936), p. 190.

16. See my *From the Beginnings of Philosophy to Plotinus,* Volume 1 of *A History of Western Philosophy,* Notre Dame, 1963, pp. 222-8.

17. I would be less than candid if I did not point out that Aristotle sometimes (*Metaphysics,* 1025b25) divides philosophy into theoretical, practical and productive.

18. Consider the context of the snippet Curtius took from Grabmann: "Ad tertium dicendum quod septem liberales artes non sufficienter dividunt philosophiam theoricam, sed ideo, ut dicit Hugo de Sancto Victore in III sui *Didascalon* [sic], praetermissis quibusdam aliis, septem connumerantur, quia his primum erudiebantur, qui philisophiam discere volebant. Et ideo distinguuntur in trivium et quadrivium, 'eo quod his quasi quibusdam viis vivax animus ad secreta philosophiae introeat.' Et hoc etiam consonat verbis Philosophi in II *Metaphysicorum,* quod modus scientiae debet quaeri ante scientias; et Commentator ibidem dicit, quod logicam, quae docet modum omnium scientiarum, debet quis addiscere ante omnes alias scientias, ad quam pertinet trivium. Dicit autem in VI *Ethicorum,* quod

mathematica potest sciri a pueris, non autem physica, quae experimentum requirit. Et sic datur intelligi, quod post logicam consequenter debet mathematica addisci, ad quam pertinet quadrivium; et ita his quasi quibusdam viis praeparatur animus ad alias philosophicas disciplinas."—*In Boethii de trinitate* (ed. Wyser), q. 5, a. 1, ad 3m.

19. Curtius, *op. cit.*, p. 217.

20. *In Libros Posteriorum Analyticorum Expositio,* proemium, n. 1.

21. See *Nicomachean Ethics,* Book Six, Chapters 3 and 4.

22. *In Boethii de trin.*, q. 5, a. 1, ad 3m, in fine,

23. One can see this in the just mentioned commentary on Boethius. In article one, Thomas writes, "Sic ergo speculabili quod est obiectum scientiae speculativae, per se competit *separatio* a materia et motu . . ." Article three begins by saying that "intellectus secundum suam operationem abstrahere possit" but subsequently Thomas restricts abstraction to thinking apart what does not exist apart and separation as thinking apart what does exist apart.

24. *In Libros Posteriorum Analyticorum Expositio,* proemium, n. 3.

25. *Ibid.*, n. 4.

26. *Ibid,* n. 5.

27. These considerations fall to the *Posterior Analytics.*

28. *Ibid.*, n. 6.

29. "Quandoque vero sola existimatio declinat in aliquam partem contradictionis propter aliquam repraesentationem, ad modum quo fit homini abominatio alicuius cibi, si repraesentetur ei sub

similitudine alicuius abominabilis. Et ad hoc
ordinatur *Poetica;* nam poetae est inducere ad
aliquod virtuosum per aliquam decentem repraesentationem."—*ibid.,* n. 6.

30. See my article "The Aesthetics of Jacques Maritain," forthcoming in *Renascence.*

31. "Praeterea, scientiarum maxime differentium non
debet esse unus modus. Sed poetica, quae minimum continet veritatis, maxime differt ab ista
scientia, quae est verissima. Ergo, cum illa procedat per metaphoricas locutiones, modus hujus
scientiae non debet esse talis."—*In I Sent.,* prologus, a. 5, obj. 3.

32. *Ibid.* "Ad tertium dicendum, quod poetica scientia est de his quae propter defectum veritatis
non possunt a ratione capi; unde oportet quod
quasi quibusdam similitudinibus ratio seducatur:
theologia autem est de his quae sunt supra rationem; et ideo modus symbolicus utrique communis est, cum neutra rationi proportionetur."

33. ". . . et, quia etiam ista principia [revealed truths]
non sunt proportionata humanae rationi secundum statum viae, quae ex sensibilibus consuevit
accipere, ideo oportet ut ad eorum cognitionem
per sensibilium similitudines manuducatur: unde
oportet modum istius scientiae esse metaphoricum sive symbolicum sive parabolicum."—*ibid.,*
body of the article.

34. *Summa theologiae,* Ia, q. 1, a. 9, ad lm.

35. See *In I de anima,* lect. 1, nn. 3-6 and *In Boethii
de trin.,* q. 6.

36. *Summa theologiae,* Ia, q. 1, a. 9, c.

37. *Ibid.,* q. 13, a. 1: "Secundum igitur quod aliquid
a nobis intellectu cognosci potest, sic a nobis
potest nominari. Ostensum est autem supra quod

Deus in hac vita non potest a nobis videri per suam essentiam; sed cognoscitur a nobis ex creaturis, secundum habitudinem principii, et per modum excellentiae et remotionis. Sic igitur potest nominari a nobis ex creaturis . . ."

38. The work is found in the Thomas De Vio Cardinalis Caietanus (1469-1534), *Scripta Philosophica,* edited by Zammit and Hering, Rome, 1952. ". . . de nominum analogia in his vacationibus edere intendo," n. 1. "Completo in conventu S. Appollinaris, Papiae suburbio, die primo Septembris MCCCCXCVIII," n. 125.

39. *Summa theologiae,* Ia, q. 16, a. 6.

40. *In Iam,* q. 16, a. 6, n. VI: "Ad secundum vero dubitationem dicitur quod illa regula de analogo tradita in littera, non est universalis de omni analogiae modo: imo, proprie loquendo, ut patet I *Ethic.,* nulli analogo convenit, sed convenit nominibus *ad u m* vel *in uno* aut *ab uno,* quae nos abusive vc mus analoga . . . Esse ergo nomen aliquod secundum propriam rationem in uno tantum, est conditio nominum quae sunt *ad unum* aut *ab uno,* etc.: et non nominum proportionaliter dictorum."

41. See my *The Logic of Analogy,* Nijhoff, 1961; the discussion of Thomas in Volume 2, *A History of Western Philosophy, From Augustine to Ockham,* Notre Dame, 1969; and *Saint Thomas Aquinas,* G. K. Hall, 1978.

42. *Summa theologiae,* Ia, q. 13, a. 3.

43. *Ibid.,* sed contra est.

44. Ibid., c. "Deum cognoscimus ex perfectionibus procedentibus in creaturas ab ipso; quae quidem perfectiones in Deo sunt secundum eminentiorem modum quam in creaturis. Intellectus autem noster eo modo apprehendit eas, secundum quod

sunt in creaturis: et secundum quod apprehendit,
ita significat per nomina. In nominibus igitur
quae Deo attribuimus, est duo considerare, scili-
cet, perfectiones ipsas significatas, ut bonitatem,
vitam, et huiusmodi; et modum significandi.
Quantum igitur ad id quod significant huiusmodi
nomina, proprie competunt Deo, et magis proprie
quam ipsis creaturis, et per prius dicuntur de eo.
Quantum vero ad modum significandi, non pro-
prie dicuntur de Deo: habent enim modum
significandi qui creaturis competit."

45. *Summa contra gentiles*, I, cap. 30.

46. *Q.D. de potentia*, q. 7, a. 5, ad 8m: "Similiter
consideranda sunt in creaturis quaedam secun-
dum quae Deo similantur, quae quantum ad rem
significatam, nullam imperfectionem important,
sicut esse, vivere et intelligere et huiusmodi; et
ista proprie dicuntur de Deo, immo per prius de
ipso et eminentius quam de creaturis. Quaedam
vero sunt secundum quae creatura differt a Deo,
consequentia ipsam prout est ex nihilo, sicut
potentialitas, privatio, motus et alia huiusmodi:
et ista sunt falsa de Deo. Et quaecumque nomina
in sui intellectu conditiones huiusmodi claudunt,
de Deo dici non possunt nisi metaphorice, sicut
leo, lapis et huiusmodi, propter hoc quod in sui
definitione habent materiam."

47. Thomas takes over from Pseudo-Dionysius, a
three-stage approach to the divine names. ". . .
tripliciter ista de Deo dicuntur. Primo quidem
affirmative, ut dicamus, Deus est sapiens; quod
quidem de eo oportet dicere propter hoc quod
est in eo similitudo sapientiae ab ipso fluentis:
quia tamen non est in Deo sapientia qualem nos
intelligimus et nominamus, potest vere negari,
ut dicatur, Deus non est sapiens. Rursum quia
sapientia non negatur de Deo quia ipse deficiat

a sapientia, sed quia supereminentius est in ipso quam dicatur aut intelligatur, ideo oportet dicere quod Deus sit supersapiens."

48. See my "Metaphor and Analogy," in *Inquiries into Medieval Philosophy,* ed. James F. Ross, Greenwood Publishing, Westport, Conn., 1971.

49. *Ibid.* pp. 87-90.

50. This spectrum was suggested to me by the essay "The Immediate Stages of the Erotic," in Volume One of Kierkegaard's *Either/Or,* Princeton, 1959.

51. University of California Press, 1971, "Words Set Free," pp. 121-144.

52. Think of the etymology of *verbum* in *verberatio.* Cf. *Q. D. de Veritate,* q. 4, a. 1, ad 8m.

53. J. L. Austin, *How to Do Things with Words,* Oxford, 1965; John R. Searle, *SpeechActs,* Cambridge, 1969.

54. The administration of the sacraments involves performative utterances. Cf. *Summa theologiae,* IIIa, q. 60, a. 7 and 8.

55. *Topics,* Book One, chapter 2.

56. *Nicomachean Ethics,* Book One, chapter 3.

57. Iris Murdoch, *The Sovereignty of the Good,* Schocken Books, New York, 1971. Notre Dame University Press will soon publish MacIntyre's *After Virtue.*

58. Jacques Maritain, *Art et scolastique,* Paris, 1920, pp. 17 ff.

59. *Q. D. de veritate,* q. 11, a. 4.

60. Indiana University Press, 1954.

61. Doubleday Anchor Book, New York, 1953.

62. *Ibid.,* p. 17.

63. *Ibid.,* p. 18.

64. Paul Claudel, *Oeuvres en Prose*, Bibliotheque de la Pléiade, Paris, 1965, p. 439 ff.
65. M. D. Chenu, *Introduction à l'étude de Saint Thomas d'Aquin*, Paris, 1954, p. 98 ff.
66. Josef Pieper, *Guide to Thomas Aquinas*, New York, 1962.
67. Ibid., p. 109.

Published by the Marquette University Press
Milwaukee, Wisconsin 53233
United States of America

#1 St. Thomas and the Life of Learning (1937)
by John F. McCormick, S.J. (1874-1943)
professor of philosophy, Loyola University.
                                ISBN 0-87462-101-1

#2 St. Thomas and the Gentiles (1938) by Morti-
mer J. Adler, Ph.D., Director of the Insti-
tute of Philosophical Research, San Francisco,
Calif.   ISBN 0-87462-102-X

#3 St. Thomas and the Greeks (1939) by Anton
C. Pegis, Ph.D., professor of philosophy,
Pontifical Institute of Mediaeval Studies,
Toronto.   ISBN 0-87462-103-8

#4 The Nature and Functions of Authority (1940)
by Yves Simon, Ph.D., (1903-1961) profes-
sor of philosophy of social thought, Univer-
sity of Chicago.   ISBN 0-87462-104-6

#5 St. Thomas and Analogy (1941) by Gerald B.
Phelan, Ph.D., (1892-1965) professor of phi-
losophy, St. Michael's College, Toronto.
                                ISBN 0-87462-105-4

#6 St. Thomas and the Problem of Evil (1942) by
Jacques Maritain, Ph.D., professor *emeritus*
of philosophy, Princeton University.
                                ISBN 0-87462-106-2

#7 Humanism and Theology (1943) by Werner
Jaeger, Ph.D., Litt.D., (1888-1961) Univer-
sity professor, Harvard University.
                                ISBN 0-87462-107-0

#8 The Nature and Origins of Scientism (1944) by John Wellmuth, Chairman of the Department of Philosophy, Loyola University.
ISBN 0-87462-108-9

#9 Cicero in the Courtroom of St. Thomas Aquinas (1945) by E. K. Rand, Ph.D., Litt D., LL.D. (1871-1945) Pope professor of Latin, *emeritus,* Harvard University.   ISBN 0-87462-109-7

#10 St. Thomas and Epistemology (1946) by Louis-Marie Regis, O.P., Th.L., Ph.D., director of the Albert the Great Institute of Mediaeval Studies, University of Montreal.
ISBN 0-87462-110-0

#11 St. Thomas and the Greek Moralists (1947, Spring) by Vernon J. Bourke, Ph.D., professor of philosophy, St. Louis University, St. Louis, Missouri.   ISBN 0-87462-111-9

#12 History of Philosophy and Philosophical Education (1947, Fall) by Etienne Gilson of the *Académie français,* director of studies and professor of the history of Mediaeval philosophy, Pontifical Institute of Mediaeval Studies, Toronto.   ISBN 0-87462-112-7

#13 The Natural Desire for God (1948) by William R. O'Connor, S.T.L., Ph.D., former professor of dogmatic theology, St. Joseph's Seminary, Dunwoodie, N.Y.   ISBN 0-87462-113-5

#14 St. Thomas and the World State (1949) by Robert M. Hutchins, former Chancellor of the University of Chicago, president, of the Fund for the Republic.   ISBN 0-87462-114-3

#15 Method in Metaphysics (1950) by Robert J. Henle, S.J., Ph.D., academic vice-president, St. Louis University, St. Louis, Missouri.
ISBN 0-87462-115-1

#16 Wisdom and Love in St. Thomas Aquinas (1951) by Etienne Gilson of the *Académie français*, director of studies and professor of the history of Mediaeval philosophy, Pontifical Institute of Mediaeval Studies, Toronto.
ISBN 0-87462-116-X

#17 The Good in Existential Metaphysics (1952) by Elizabeth G. Salmon, Ph.D., professor of philosophy in the graduate school, Fordham University.
ISBN 0-87462-117-8

#18 St. Thomas and the Object of Geometry (1953) by Vincent Edward Smith, Ph.D., director, Philosophy of Science Institute, St. John's University.
ISBN 0-87462-118-6

#19 Realism and Nominalism Revisited (1954) by Henry Veatch, Ph.D., professor and chairman of the department of philosophy, Northwestern University.
ISBN 0-87462-119-4

#20 Imprudence in St. Thomas Aquinas (1955) by Charles J. O'Neil, Ph.D., professor of philosophy, Villanova University.
ISBN 0-87462-120-8

#21 The Truth That Frees (1956) by Gerard Smith, S.J., Ph.D., professor of philosophy, Marquette University.
ISBN 0-87462-121-6

#22 St. Thomas and the Future of Metaphysics (1957) by Joseph Owens, C.Ss.R., Ph.D., professor of philosophy, Pontifical Institute of Mediaeval Studies, Toronto.
ISBN 0-87462-122-4

#23 Thomas and the Physics of 1958: A Confrontation (1958) by Henry Margenau, Ph.D., Eugene Higgins professor of physics and natural philosophy, Yale University.
ISBN 0-87462-123-2

#24 Metaphysics and Ideology (1959) by Wm. Oliver Martin, Ph.D., professor of philosophy, University of Rhode Island.
ISBN 0-87462-124-0

#25 Language, Truth and Poetry (1960) by Victor M. Hamm, Ph.D., professor of English, Marquette University. ISBN 0-87462-125-9

#26 Metaphysics and Historicity (1961) by Emil L. Fackenheim, Ph.D., professor of philosophy, University of Toronto.
ISBN 0-87462-126-7

#27 The Lure of Wisdom (1962) by James D. Collins, Ph.D., professor of philosophy, St. Louis University. ISBN 0-87462-127-5

#28 Religion and Art (1963) by Paul Weiss, Ph.D. Sterling professor of philosophy, Yale University. ISBN 0-87462-128-3

#29 St. Thomas and Philosophy (1964) by Anton C. Pegis, Ph.D., professor of philosophy, Pontifical Institute of Mediaeval Studies, Toronto. ISBN 0-87462-129-1

#30 The University in Process (1965) by John O. Riedl, Ph.D., dean of faculty, Queensboro Community College. ISBN 0-87462-130-5

#31 The Pragmatic Meaning of God (1966) by Robert O. Johann, associate professor of philosophy, Fordham University.
ISBN 0-87462-131-3

#32 Religion and Empiricism (1967) by John E. Smith, Ph.D., professor of philosophy, Yale University. ISBN 0-87462-132-1